I0756240

FINISHING LINE PRESS
www.finishinglinepress.com

Not Just Us

poems by

Eleanor Berry

Finishing Line Press
Georgetown, Kentucky

Not Just Us

ISBN 979-8-89990-456-1 First Edition

ACKNOWLEDGMENTS

Grateful acknowledgment is made to the editors of the following publications, in which the listed poems first appeared, some in different versions:

The Anthology of New England Writers: "Every Corner"
Hawai'i Pacific Review: "The Woodcarver on the Animals He Rejected for His Ark"
Moving Mountain: "To a Sheep Loose on I-5"
The Raven Chronicles: "A Coral Polyp Considers the Nature of Its Identity"
The Oregonian: "Your Final July"
Verseweavers: The Oregon State Poetry Association Anthology of Prize-winning Poems: "The Jackdaws at Stonehenge"
Windfall: A Journal of Poetry of Place: "The Old Desk and the Antelope"

"*Misto*" was included in the 2018 Paint the Town / Write the Town exhibit at Elsinore Framing and Fine Arts Gallery, Salem, OR.

Publisher: Leah Huete de Maines
Editor: Christen Kincaid
Cover Art: "The Natural Order of Things" by Bethany Rowland
Author Photo: Richard Berry
Cover Design: Elizabeth Maines McCleavy

Order online: www.finishinglinepress.com
also available on amazon.com

Author inquiries and mail orders:
Finishing Line Press
PO Box 1626
Georgetown, Kentucky 40324
USA

Contents

for Richard and for
the animal kin who have
entered our lives and let us
enter theirs

In Haberdashery

after a statuette signed "David Sharp, Rye, Eng."

This badger is dapper in aqua morning-coat and vest
over tan, russet-checked trousers, with matching
russet-on-tan polkadot tie knotted at his throat.

Statuette barely a foot high, he stands erect, braced
by a broad tail. Long, blunt-tipped snout, white blaze
from nose to crown, belies his finery.

Cast-molded figurine bought, years back,
for a gift to my father, reclaimed after his death—
I picked it for him because I saw it as his image

of himself: fierce, fossorial hermit passing for
a country gentleman, perfectly outfitted
in the fashion of an earlier era.

Now he peers sidelong from the mantelpiece,
an animal in haberdashery. Like me, like you.

How They See Us

like a white snail
in the supple dark flowers
—Earle Birney

How curiously made
we two humans must appear
to the four alpacas who live
in our pasture and barn—each of us,
such a poor, bare, forked
animal as Lear on the heath
saw every man to be, once stripped
of the trappings of rank.

How curiously clad
we must appear—not
in coats that grow from the skin,
covering all but the toes, insensibly
thickening from week
to week, blanket
against cold, when wet
shingled to shed rain—but

in sundry assorted pieces,
different each day, offhandedly
sloughed, later as casually resumed,
leaving patches of skin
bare, leaving the face
naked, yet—equally odd—
keeping the two feet
always shod.

How frightening they must find
our arms and hands that move
ways their forelegs never will:
now drawn in, now spread wide—
spokes from the hub of our trunks,

fearsomely wheeling about,
reaching and, with curling fingers,
grasping like mouths.

How strange the ways we arrange
our limbs must look
to these kin of camels, when they see
us lower our bodies, not,
right down to the ground,
as they do cushing—folding
front legs under, tucking
the back ones up behind—but just

setting our rumps
on platforms of sorts.
They whose swan necks
remain erect while they
lie prone, who wrestle
by twining those necks
together like snakes—
what do they make

of our heads' short stalks?
They who keep silent except
to hum in distress, shriek
warning or challenge—
what do they make
of our tireless talk, the multifarious
sounds we pour out
at them, at each other, at the air?

When we smile, showing
upper incisors where they
have a dental pad, do they think
we're baring our teeth,
like coyotes, to snap?

We never join them chewing cud—
how can they tell that we, too,
ruminate, after a fashion?

How do they see us
when we come among them?
Squatting amid cushed alpacas,
how do we see ourselves?
A mirror, if one were hanging
on the barn wall, would show us
as clumsy clowns in motley
beside their furred and limber grace.

Offerings: A Monologue Addressed to Marianne Moore

> *… the ancient Egyptian language had no word for "animal" as a separate category ….*
>
> —Eric A. Powell, "Messengers to the Gods,"
> *Archaeology*, March/April 2014

Right there, in your Brooklyn,
in the storage vaults
of its museum where you often viewed
artifacts you admired and made
the subjects of poems:
thirty boxes left untouched
seven decades since their purchase
circa 1940. You
were a regular visitor then—
did you read of the acquisition
in a museum brochure?

You would have marveled to see
the contents of those boxes, only now
opened to light—animal mummies
from a time of turbulence
in ancient Egypt. Cats, dogs, hawks,
ibises, sundry other creatures.
Some elaborately wrapped, realistic detail
on their heads; some simply sheathed
in strips of linen.

Those wrappings now pierced
by X-rays, some prove to contain
complete remains, limbs tenderly arranged;
others turn out to cover
a single bone, a wing, a bundle of feathers;
still others, a jumble
of ill-assorted bodies.

Whether true or not to what they enclose,
some wrappings themselves would delight you:
the contours of a cat's head
meticulously preserved, its face given
a wide-eyed expression, eerily alive;
the long-billed head of an ibis
projecting from a perfectly symmetrical
two-tone, basket-woven body-sheath,
an exuberance of ornament topping
a sort of brace behind its neck.

In ancient Egyptian, no word
for *animal* apart from human—
you would relish the recognition
of commonality implicit in that absence.
Yet temples carried on
a profitable business, not without corruption,
raising creatures of various species
to mummify for sale to the pious,
anxious to placate their gods.

With fierce precision, you would note
what extant records tell:
At one temple alone,
sixty thousand living ibises at once, all
intended to be mummified and sold
to pilgrims for their offerings
to the scribe god Thoth.

Amid Freewheeling Crows

You startle me, landing on a fence post
right outside the living-room window—
your naked head, strikingly human,
but for its wattle-red hue.

Beside other birds, all fully feathered,
your kind looks as odd
as we do among other mammals,
our bare skin next to their fur.

You turkey! Vulture!
Your double name,
two words we call one another
to mock, accuse—

but you seem sympathetic,
now that I see you close.
Amid freewheeling crows, you grip
the fence post, size up the scene.

You have the bony face and bald pate
of a lean, old, beak-nosed man,
and your restless gaze
is wary, puzzled, troubled.

It's a long time
before you lift off, beating
broad wings to bear aloft
your heavy body.

Every Corner

1

As she explained how the operation had gone,
the veterinary surgeon's slender hands flexed and curved
to show the irregular mass of the tumor,
how it was attached by a stalk to the fourth rib,
how she had to cut the third rib as well
to lift it out. That night, in one of the dreams
of a fitful sleep, I watched a young woman, slight
and sinewy like the surgeon, learning to skate.
Within minutes, she was moving with such grace
I couldn't stop staring, as avid to follow
her every motion as to watch a deer, surprised at grazing,
bound the length of the pasture toward the cover of woods.

2

The heat turned down for the night,
blower finally shut off, in the stillness we hear
the heating ducts bong as they cool,
and the hot-water pipes, as they, too, cool
after toothbrushing and evening bath. We hear
our big dog, home from the animal hospital
where a malignant tumor was cut from his chest,
shift on his dog-bed, his heavy body thump
against the wall. We hear him whimper,
struggle up, limp to every corner
of the room in turn, as if one
would hold comfort.

Sighting

A sudden thunk against a dining-room window—
some headlong flier the hawk silhouettes
taped on the panes failed to frighten away. Stunned,
the victim—about the size of a jay—dangles
a moment by one yellow, three-toed foot
from a twig in the hydrangeas, winter-bare
beneath the windows. Then the curled toes
lose their hold. The body drops
the rest of the way to the ground, lies
upside down in the dirt, eyes closed,
feathered chest heaving.

But scarcely a minute later,
the eyes blink open, swivel around. The disheveled bird
rights itself, lifts off, wings over the backyard
to the woodlot behind, lands near the top
of a Douglas fir. It stays there a long time,
perched on a high bough, slowly turning its head
to look all around, though it doesn't seem to see
my husband and me, watching with binoculars
through the window it just struck.

Speckled breast. Flat, round face. A compact
bird of prey. We compare it to the plates
in Peterson, Sibley, check field marks and range,
find a perfect match: *northern pygmy owl.*
If it hadn't smashed into our window,
we might never have encountered
this small, strong-winged hunter, even though
it's active in daylight. Aloft on a high branch,
no more than a knob to the naked eye—
had we noticed it at all, we'd likely have thought it
a lump of moss. How little we know
what others inhabit this place
we call ours.

The Unicorn Alone

From her forehead, one long, spiral-ridged horn
extends straight up. The other,
broken at the base, dangles
loosely down.

No mythical beast, the unicorn
is *Taurotragus oryx*, an eland,
largest African antelope,
of great bulk, so massive and tall that,
moving through firs, pale hide
flashing between dark trunks, she exceeds
the myth. Seeing you approach, she looks
directly at you, *docile, inoffensive,*
eyes uncertain
whether to trust.

                    At any sudden sound—
engine backfire, tire blowout,
door slammed, even a handclap—
she jumps, pivots, trots
the length of the pasture in a few
swift strides, sails   *in spite of bulk*
a good jumper   over the fence, disappears
into dense woods beyond.

No mythical beast, her hooves
poke deep holes in woodlot duff,
in pasture, lawn, garden dirt.
Beside her hoofprints in the flowerbed,
the iris fans are bitten off
clean at the base. Along the path
to the barn, brown ball bearings,
piled and strewn—her scat.

This marginal farmland, where tillable soil
gives way to orchard and pasture, these
grade into timber, offers
much the same mix—grass, browse, and cover—
as the land   *bush or veld, acacia savanna,*
miombo woodland   half the globe away
where her kind is native, though the plants
are different here, and
the winters colder.

By nature *gregarious, in herds of a few*
to thirty or forty, she is alone,
her mate and sisters rustled   *easily*
captured and killed, yields
large amounts of tender meat, thick hide
is excellent   from their corral to become
exotic game for domestic safaris. Left
behind for worthless because
of her broken horn, she is bereft
even of her calf, curled tight against
a tree when lightning flayed its trunk
clean of bark.

                              Forlorn, she roams
this patchwork of foothill farms, seeking,
it seems, her lost ones, or at least
kindred creatures to befriend. Finding
pastured alpacas, protected within
a ring of predator fence she could
clear without effort, she grazes
close outside, then lies
pressed to the fencewire, chewing cud
in afternoon sun, returns each day.

As the legend tells, there is a lady,
sole human the unicorn trusts
comes eagerly to the lap
of the maid, whose delicate hand
rests on his mane   Slender and small,
as the tapestries show, but no
virgin, attracting the unicorn
by her purity. Instead,
a middle-aged woman, single mother
with grown children, no money to fence
an antelope so large. *Uni*
comes to her call.

                                        Not at any
hunter's bidding, she tamed
this unicorn. But she knows
the tameness makes her eland
easy prey, fears every day
to find the gentle creature shot. Every day
she comes in her battered van, bringing
alfalfa hay, grain, fresh
fruit and greens, a dozen
donut holes. The lone eland savors
the succulent feed and the sweets, stays
by the van till she leaves, but
will not follow her back
across the highway to the barn and corral
empty of her kin.

The Jackdaws at Stonehenge

Three motorways converge beneath
this grassy hill, crowned with the ancient ring
of standing stones. Cars, lorries, buses speed
north and south, east and west. Wind whips
around the stones, flattens the spring grass

on the brow of the hill. Chill gusts pierce
our coats and caps, as we walk
in procession the circular path. Our photographs
will show no motorways or fellow tourists, only
gray monoliths against turbulent sky,

will show only as black specks the jackdaws,
crows in gray cowls, pecking around the base
of the slabs, flying in and out of nest-holes
eroded in the stone. Whatever they were
to humans once, these stones are home

to jackdaws now—placid community oblivious
to the traffic below the hill, to the daily
processions of gawkers with guidebooks
that make no mention of them, fluffing
their feathers against the cold spring wind.

In That Country

Robin has finally sold her large painting
of a shepherd cradling a lamb in his arms.
She's happy it went to a woman unaccustomed
to buying original art, who said she needed
that painting—one of Robin's
biggest pieces and almost the only
figure study among her many
brilliantly colored floral still lifes
and northwest landscapes. She retells
with relish a story the woman shared
of meeting a shepherdess abroad:

Making conversation, the woman had told
the shepherdess how a neighbor's goats
had gotten out and eaten her garden.
"But wasn't someone with them?"
the shepherdess had asked, confused.
In her country, animals were never
left by themselves. *In that country,*
Robin adds for emphasis, *people*
live with their animals.

Every evening, trailed by a mixed-breed dog
with one blind eye, Robin takes water and feed
to an aged pot-bellied pig; a half dozen geese,
whom she shuts for the night in a shed, to keep them
safe from coyotes; a young donkey, who brays
like a foghorn as Robin comes near, lugging
a full pail; five goats, five different breeds, all
butting each other to get to the biggest
piles of feed; and a trio of llamas—Joyful, the oldest,
gets medicine for arthritis mixed with his food.
Back at the house, two miniature poodles
yip and leap for attention. On the cluttered
sunporch, three cats weave between easel,
exercycle, and easy chair. And on the deck,

crowded with potted plants, all demanding
regular care, two doves—one twenty years old—
wait in their cage for Robin to come
soothing with her soft voice.

To a Sheep Loose on I-5

Your white wedge of a face
yanks my startled gaze
from the roadway ahead to the lanes
opposite—you're cutting a swift
diagonal across them, heading right
for the median between us. The swinging
bulk of your shaggy winter fleece
overweights your trotting matchstick legs.

The oncoming cars and semis
brake to a stop. A couple of pick-ups
pull onto the shoulder. A man
zigzags after you across
the lanes of backed-up traffic. What
do you make of it all—the strange ground
your hooves don't seem to dent, the growling
engines, thickening fumes, the shouts?

All your life, while you've cropped
tender grass amid your kin,
freeway traffic has racketed past
your fenced home fields. But surely
you aren't prepared to find it
bearing down on you. From behind
the fence, it must have seemed
an endless stampede that never
swerved your way. And from inside
the barn, where your flock bedded down,
close-crowded, roofed from the rain, breathing
the familiar stench of damp wool,
hay, packed dirt, and dung,
it must have seemed no threat
at all, just a torrent that kept
to its channel. Now, I guess,

you must be seeing a pack
of giant, steel-clad wolves, glaring,
teeth bared, braced to run you down.

Already your looming face
has shrunk to a pinpoint
in my rearview mirror.

Your Final July

for Bix

While you lie close by in the grass, joints too stiff,
breath too short, for the walk we're used to taking

this time every day, I dig out the hydrangea that died
from the heat last summer.

Its taproot is cable-thick, lodged deep;
lateral roots, tough wires, twisted and thrust

in among stones. Sweat stings my scalp and neck,
rivulets down my chest. I pry with the spade,

jostle the knobby stump to loosen its hold on the soil
enough I can wrench it out. But this shrub

is as obstinately rooted, dead,
as, still alive, it was stubbornly dying.

The Old Desk and the Antelope

The hulk of a desk my husband and I
bought secondhand forty years back, then
hauled wherever we moved, lies on its side
gutted of drawers, legs stiffly out.
Its massive top lies flat on the carpet nearby.
Every bent, rusted nail some past owner
clumsily drove in, my husband will pry out.
Every age-weakened joint in drawers and frame
he will pull apart, seal with fresh glue,
and clamp tight till the glue has dried.

When the desk is stood back upright, its top
screwed back on, and its drawers slid
back onto their runners, now waxed smooth,
it will be sturdier than it ever was
the four decades it served to hold, first,
a manual typewriter, then a series of computers,
always piles of papers and books. Sound
as it must have left the factory, it will become
bill-paying desk in the corner space
we've cleared for it, where it fits exactly.

~

The huge antelope that has roamed,
for several years now, the land hereabout,
adopting our pasture for base, lies on her side,
eyes glazed over, legs stiffly out.
Beside the massive, lifeless body,
a slender woman, the eland's owner, kneels
sobbing in the frozen grass, strokes
and strokes with her small hands
the vast flanks. Her daily rounds—searching out
the beloved creature who leapt any fence,
bringing her water and feed—have ended
the way she feared they would.

What mercy could do
her son's rifle shot to the heart
and follow-up pistol to the brain
have done, ending the eland's pain
from the arrow aimed by malice or mistake,
lodged deep in her chest.
The son will return with a trailer, winch
the three-quarter-ton carcass aboard,
haul it home, and with a backhoe dig a grave
long and wide and deep enough to hold it.

In our garden, the perennials
the wandering antelope grazed
again and again to the roots,
the shrubs and saplings she browsed
again and again down to a stub of trunk,
will grow back untouched, profusely branch.

The Arctic Fox

After Marianne Moore, "The Arctic Ox (or Goat)"

Derived from "The Wanderer," by Garry Hamilton, in the February/March 2012 issue of *National Wildlife*

About the Arctic fox
Miss Moore says simply that
  to wear its fur, one has to kill it,
whereas she prefers to dress
in fiber creatures yield without distress—

like qiviut, the underwool
the musk-ox sheds each spring.
  Fur aside, I think the Arctic fox
an animal whose curious traits
Moore would have found as worthy of praise

as those she eulogized in the pangolin,
jerboa, and sundry other creatures.
  Surely she would have celebrated how—
like plants that adapt to desert weather
by hunkering low and retaining water

in leaves reduced to tabs,
thickened and densely fuzzed—
  the Arctic fox has fur on its footpads
to preserve body heat while it hunts
on polar ice swept by frigid gusts

and cocks stubbier ears,
sniffs out prey with a shorter muzzle,
  than its cousins whose range is temperate.
When the local lemming population
crashes, it survives this decimation

of accessible prey, not by hibernating
but by roaming through the three-month
  Arctic night, seeking

what polar bears leave of their kill
once those top predators have eaten their fill,

ice-tombed carcasses of walrus or whale,
new-born seal pups in frozen lairs—
        whatever food circumstance may provide.
Even on sea ice, featureless and in constant motion,
the Arctic fox can tell direction,

traces complex routes that may extend
two, even three, thousand miles,
        but still loop back to a former den.
This compact creature has adapted well
to the harsh, unstable place it dwells.

But even if we wear no fur,
are we not still killing the Arctic fox
        by consuming goods whose manufacture
emits pollutants that insulate Earth,
so shrink the polar icecap, and lure

the larger red fox north?
Facing competition
        and reduction of its range at once,
may not the Arctic fox be pressed beyond
its power, however remarkable, to respond?

To the Last Bramble Cay Melomys

Australian researchers say rising sea levels have wiped out a rodent that lived on a tiny outcrop in the Great Barrier Reef, in what they say is the first documented extinction of a mammal species due to human-caused climate change.
—*New York Times*, 14 June 2016

Did you know you were the only one left?

Had you watched your siblings starve or drown?
Had you waited, or wandered seeking,
in vain for a mate? Had you searched in vain
for succulent purslane, for crevices where
you could curl safe in sleep?

You must have found the plants dead
in every spot you once had munched fresh leaves.
You couldn't have known what killed them,
couldn't have known that rising seas
had poisoned what soil they hadn't washed away.

You must have cowered
through frequent, violent storms.
You couldn't have known that storms had become
more frequent and more violent
than your kind had ever experienced before

in the million years they'd evolved to fit
perfectly the compact habitat
of a ten-acre outcrop of coral reef.
Even if fear of people had passed down
to you from ancestors that survived

when European sailors shot the "rats"
they found on Bramble Cay, you had no way to know
that humans living high on vast lands
were destroying by their profligate habits
your low-lying islet home, your sole place on Earth.

A Coral Polyp Considers the Nature of Its Identity

I am connected by a thin sheet of tissue
to other polyps identical to me. I am
one member of a dynamic collectivity of clones.
Together, we form a bulwark, sheltering
the edge of the land from the battering sea.

Although as fixed in place as any rock formation
or rooted plant, I am a predatory animal.
I am a stomach, a mouth, and tentacles.
Coiled within my skin are spring-
loaded stingers that shoot poison darts into my prey.

I host a crowd of minuscule creatures, some dwelling
in my mucus coat, some inside my endodermal cells.
All pay their rent in kind: The food they manufacture
they share with me. Defending themselves,
they save me from disease.

They are my farmers and my armies. I depend upon them.
If their crops fail, if their troops fall to invading throngs,
I die. So it is for all of us polyp clones—
if our microbes cease to nourish and protect us, we succumb.
This living reef, built of our bodies, begins to crumble away.

What am I? Am I an *I?* … If not an *I*,
then what? … I'm not myself alone—I'm nothing
apart from my neighbors and my tenants.
We, all of us together, compose a *holobiont*:
a great chorus where none can sing solo.

And you, smug reader, supposing yourself
sole and entire—you are no such thing. You, too,
live by what lives around and within you.

Amid Kin

Each morning we wake encircled by animals—
two cats curled and purring, dozens more creatures
that do not move or breathe, yet have
stances of conscious life. It seems as if they all
have kept watch while we slept.

Sewn, carved, molded, blown,
shaped from wood, metal, stone, glass, glazed and unglazed
ceramic, plastic, grass, wool, cotton, hide, synthetic fiber … pigs
from every place we've traveled and from friends
who've found them for us gaze out from each shelf
of the curio cabinet, stand, sit, and sprawl about the bedroom.
A footstool, a whistle, a vessel, a change purse, a brooch, a tie clip,
a charm …
only a couple are banks. By far the most are pure figures
of intelligent, sensuous life.

They're hardly alone. On bureau and
lamptable,
on a child's miniature Windsor chair, resides a whole company
of creatures: three stuffed bears, two alpacas and a llama, a terrier
sitting as if for a treat, a generic dog improbably blue who can
only flop,
a platypus, a tiger, a moose. On shelves beside decorative
handpainted plates
and an antique vase, sit a dainty cat of cobalt glass and a plump
one of silver,
a gilt-edged china terrier, a blown-glass pair of baby birds, a
plastic horse
no bigger than the birds, a ceramic polar bear equally small
resting on his haunches. A quirky peaceable kingdom.

And on
the walls—
five Holsteins in acrylics lying under an oak, three sheep in oil
huddled on a hill, "Bix and Bob resting under trees" (their photos
collaged

in a painting of their graves on our land), a white alpaca
grazing
in a dusky watercolor meadow, two plump white chickens
perched on a red
wheelbarrow, a wingèd pig coming in for a landing right over
our bed.

We've gathered them all, drawn them close around us—
our farmyard, our forest. Here indoors, we lie down amid
kin.
They hold us through each night, carry us back into day.

Misto
July 2018

Five decades ago, it constellated in the developer bath—
print of two sandwiched negatives, matched portraits
of you and me. Every stronger feature, yours or mine,
prevailed over its weaker version, so the composite face
had the aspect of a god—strong brow and strong jaw,
straight nose, firm mouth, direct gaze.
The You-Me we called it.

                                        I think of it now, meeting
this young offspring of an alpaca and a llama, perfect
in every feature and proportion, combining
the beauties of one parent with those of the other.
Neither llama nor alpaca, and not a cross between
a male llama and female alpaca—not a *huarizo*.
Instead, this rarer creature, with an alpaca for sire
and a llama for dam—a *misto*. Both elegant
and robust, with the queenly eyelashes of her mother
and her father's sturdy build.

                                        I think of it again—
the You-Me—when *Time* arrives in the mail
with another composite face on its cover, another pair
of sandwiched portraits: Vladimir Putin and
Donald Trump. In this computer superimposition,
the juts and slopes of each man's visage
have been evened out, blended into a uniform
bland coldness, power without character.

Misto—mixture where strength adds to strength,
beauty to beauty, in a new harmony
of beauty and strength. Can it survive?
Can it reproduce? Can it overcome
the redoubling of crassness, venality, and greed,
the multiplication of hate and fear?

What Song

June 2020

> *Solitary the thrush,*
> *The hermit withdrawn to himself, avoiding the settlements,*
> *Sings by himself a song.*
> —Walt Whitman

Hermit thrush, your voice of longing
used to rise each spring
from thickets and overgrown orchards,
from decades-old rows of planted pines
on the Great Lakes migratory flyway
where we once lived.

Now we are long gone
from there to a far corner
of the country, and the rewilding farms
where your kind could rest and feed
now are subdivided and developed, even as
it takes a longer flight to reach
breeding spots that aren't too warm.

In memory only
can we hear
the notes of longing
in your song—

notes a grieving poet summoned
to undergird his solemn chant, remembering
the slow, ceremonious journey
of Lincoln's coffin across
the springtime land
freshly, deeply
wounded in war.

What bird now
can give voice
to the pain of this land?
What song
can sound its grief?

The Woodcarver on the Animals He Rejected for His Ark

These are the ones who, when I told them,
"Find a partner, form a double line," simply
ignored me. The hare and the tortoise
went on with their race. The pair of T-rexes
kept sniggering over some joke they shared.

The snake kept doing his inchworm imitation—
humping up and down, instead of slithering
side to side along the ground. The fox,
catching a scent, raced away. The giraffe stood lookout
for the elephant—they were clearly up to something.

The moose hung back, gazing wistfully
at her sad face in a pool. The green frog
stayed rapt in conversation with the bear,
wouldn't budge till she'd finished her say.
The blue whale spouted, then dived deeper.

Noah would have wanted nothing to do
with the likes of these—willful, wayward,
intent on their own agendas. But could it be,
they're the very sort who'd have the vision needed
to build a new world from the wreckage of the old?

Unpeopled

Between high ridge and flat lake, this width
of tawny grass and brush: a place on earth—
on Earth, on this planet Earth.

In such a place,
you know the human world is not the world. You see
how manifold the world would be

without us.

Notes

"The Unicorn Alone" incorporates text from writings about the habitat and characteristics of elands and from ones about the legend of the unicorn as represented in the Unicorn Tapestries housed in The Cloisters museum in Manhattan.

Bramble Cay ("To the Last Bramble Cay Melomys") is a small, vegetated coral island at the northern end of the Great Barrier Reef. The Bramble Cay melomys is a recently extinct rodent endemic to the island.

The features referred to in the persona poem "A Coral Polyp Considers the Nature of Its Identity" are mostly attributes common to Anthozoa, the class of Cnidaria to which coral belong.

Eleanor Berry's most recent poetry collection, *Works of Wildfire*, won the 2022 Grayson Books Chapbook Award. Previous publications include *Green November* (Traprock Books, 2007), *No Constant Hues* (Turnstone Books of Oregon, 2015), and *Only So Far* (Main Street Rag, 2019). A past president of the Oregon Poetry Association and the National Federation of State Poetry Societies, Berry holds a Ph.D. from the University of Toronto and taught literature and writing at colleges and universities in Milwaukee, Wisconsin, as well as Willamette University in Salem, Oregon. Over several decades, she has been active in organizing community literary and arts activities everywhere she has lived.

www.ingramcontent.com/pod-product-compliance
Lightning Source LLC
LaVergne TN
LVHW090539110826
845146LV00003B/1188

* 9 7 9 8 8 9 9 9 0 4 5 6 1 *